My Great-Grandmother's Book of Ferns

ANCESTORS
IN THE ATTIC

My Great-Grandmother's
Book of Ferns

MICHAEL HOLROYD

PIMPERNEL
PRESS LTD
www.pimpernelpress.com

Pimpernel Press Limited
www.pimpernelpress.com

ANCESTORS IN THE ATTIC
My Great-Grandmother's Book of Ferns
© Pimpernel Press Limited 2017
Text and illustrations © Michael Holroyd 2017

A catalogue record for this book is available from the British Library.

Designed by Anne Wilson
Typeset in Addington

ISBN 978-1-910258-84-2

Printed and bound in China
by C&C Offset Printing Company Limited

9 8 7 6 5 4 3 2 1

Frontispiece: The initials 'A.E.H.' on the front cover of the *Book of Ferns*

Contents

FOREWORD

M ichael Holroyd explains how his family, among many other expatriates, settled in India during the nineteenth century. At that time the ladies of the families, and sometimes their husbands too, had time on their hands and one leisure occupation was the study of the local fauna and flora. With the aid of a series of beautifully prepared sheets of pressed fern fronds collected and pressed by his great-grandmother, Anne Eliza Holroyd, Michael Holroyd has explored the life of his family in India and back home in the United Kingdom in the mid- to late nineteenth century. His research sadly revealed that at the young age of thirty, Anne Eliza committed suicide; but her album of ferns survives in excellent condition after many years lost in the attic of the former family home. It reveals a fascinating story which will surely captivate readers, especially when they examine the splendid reproductions of the album pages in this book.

Expatriates compiled albums in New Zealand, Australia, Jamaica, India, and elsewhere – but usually within the British Empire. Some collected ferns, tying in nicely with the fern craze that was fashionable at that time back in Britain. A few Indian army wives produced fern albums commercially; the albums of one of them, Mrs Phoebe Jaffrey, are occasionally seen today in the book trade. Mrs Jaffrey was active around 1880. It appears that Anne Eliza compiled her album a little earlier. It was not produced for sale. Few of these privately compiled albums survive today – they gradually disintegrated in attics, attacked by damp, worms, etc. – and when they do appear they are often tatty and details of their history are scarce. Anne Eliza's album is a rare survivor. Happily, quite a few commercially produced fern albums, particularly from New Zealand, do survive today. Most that I have seen have all the specimens named. Pages, or entire albums, prepared purely to show the beauty of the ferns are less common. This album is one such: it was not a fern flora. It was a decorative book.

Addressing this issue, I was asked by the publisher, Pimpernel Press, if I would be prepared to name the specimens following modern nomenclature. I agreed but once I saw the sheets I immediately realized that this was a job far beyond my abilities. I therefore sent the book to Christopher Fraser-Jenkins, who lives in Nepal and who has spent the greater part of his life studying ferns, particularly those of the subcontinent. Christopher might blush but I do not think anyone knows more about the Indian ferns than he. He has written several very learned books on the subject. Asked to provide a list of the ferns in the album he was carried away with enthusiasm for the project, and as he compiled his 'list' he added interesting anecdotes which are repeated here alongside the appropriate plate. His observations of where the fronds might have been collected contribute some background insight into the travels of Anne Eliza.

The book is now a marriage of wonderful fern arrangements with specimens all botanically named. A book which will surely satisfy both historical and pteridological interest.

The quality of the fern pressing, the delightful patterns achieved with the arrangement of the fronds and the tidy way they have been stitched to the sheets are all evidence of Anne Eliza's skill. The sensitivity of the production confirms that an artist's hand has been active. The quality is such that a professional fern mounter would have been very happy to produce work of this high standard.

Martin Rickard (President of The British Pteridological Society 1997 2001)

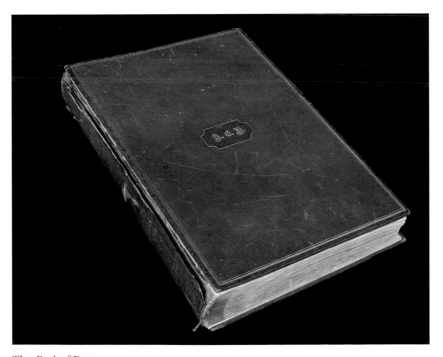

The *Book of Ferns*

The Story

THE BEGINNING OF A JOURNEY

Born in London in the late summer of 1935, I went shortly after war was declared to live in Maidenhead with my grandparents, their daughter (my aunt) and 'Old Nan', who had looked after my grandparents' three children (including my father) when they were growing up.

Compared with the great exiles and upheavals that were displacing so many families across Europe during the 1930s and 1940s, my move was negligible. Maidenhead was a mere thirty miles west of London where I had been born and passed the first four years with my parents. Yet this short move had a lasting effect on me. During childhood and early youth I saw more of my grandparents and my aunt than of my parents. This was partly because of the separation and divorce of my parents during the war and the quick appearance and disappearance of several step-parents following the end of the war. These bewildering changes were like a miniature version of the transformations that were taking place elsewhere in the world.

My grandparents were sixty years older than I was and, judging from my polite mimicry of their habits sometimes bordering on parody, I appear to have been born old. I did not begin getting younger until my late thirties, after they had died, and it was not until I was in my sixties and approaching second childhood that I began to explore my early years and understand what had controlled them.

Ours was a sombre house and the joylessness was deepened by the grim eccentricities of the family, to which I made my contribution. Every day repeated the previous day and foretold the day to come. I had the impression of reaching a full stop. We were like astronomers unable to see light and measure time before the Big Bang.

As I grew up I became used to the fact we saw no visitors – and no one saw us. The world outside was a hostile place, a battlefield. When I eventually stepped out into it – particularly at school and later during my two years' National Service in the army – I sought invisibility. To be seen was to invite trouble.

Me on my fourth birthday – about the time I went to live in Maidenhead. 'Nought
Not Out.'

During the war itself the atmosphere in our house was oddly peaceful. We knew where we were and where we belonged. We knew the enemy too. The history of Britain is crowded with wars and in retrospect we felt proud of them when we opened our history books at school. The enemy was abroad – which is the correct place for enemies if you live on an island. But in the twentieth century they were overhead as well as overseas, which was more worrying. We would hear the rising note of an air-raid warning; then silence; an explosion of bombs nearby, with our lights like giant torches searching the sky for enemy planes; and finally the long diminishing note signalling all-clear. Every day we read the headlines that other people were reading in their houses and we spoke as other people spoke about the bombs that had fallen the previous night. We did what others were doing, learning how to guard our ration books carefully and add to our rations by digging for victory in the small kitchen garden above the air-raid shelter and near the cemetery. In many ways we were ideally positioned.

It seemed as if there was only one class of people in the country, as if a sense of equality embraced us all. There was no sign of the vast gulf between rich and poor, bankers and labourers that our post-war democracy set out to create towards the end of the twentieth century. At the beginning of that century my grandfather had been rich. At the end of the war he was almost bankrupt. Many years later I realized that he had taken out a double mortgage on the house, sold much and borrowed more. There were a few cheerful interruptions, most memorably whenever a huge wooden box full of tea arrived from India. His shares in an Indian tea estate, left to him by his father, gave him moments of real pleasure. To me he seemed a scholar of tea as others were scholars of wine; the special way it must be poured was essential: and how carefully he held the cup, staring into the liquid, judging its magical properties, suddenly smiling, feeling for a moment truly at ease. As a child I watched and copied him. A cup of tea at Maidenhead was a religious vessel. My grandfather had a deep sense of loyalty to India. He had been born there and travelled back there once or twice after the war, returning much renewed.

Everyone was kind to me. My grandmother and Old Nan (who were not on speaking terms) would silently play Monopoly with me, allowing me to win. As soon as I was in my teens, my grandfather would pour me a glass of cider some evenings and, much to my delight, we would drink together, man to man. And every evening there was my magical new friend, a large television that my uncle had bought and which gave me dramatic glimpses of the extraordinary world outside, full of danger and excitement.

After the war, a strange sense of danger filled the house. Who were our enemies now? Where were our friends? We seemed to be all at sea, like a ship that had been abandoned and was drifting in mid-ocean towards the setting sun. My grandfather could not believe that Churchill, who had surely won the war for us, had been voted out of office by a Labour landslide in the general election of 1945. It did not feel as if we had won a war. Increasingly Britain was becoming a distant colony of America, which had never declared war on Hitler. We began copying everyday phrases from the United States: 'Have a nice day' and 'Enjoy!' Instead of using money to buy time and opportunity, people were using most of their time and every possible opportunity to accumulate money: it was an end in itself rather than a means to an end. Going out of doors became a risky business. We did not answer the telephone or the front door bell. Our world was indoors and we did not risk letting the enemy in. There was enough family warfare without adding strangers to it.

THE ATTIC

These were some of the memories that crowded in on me as I parked my car and stood on the pavement looking at our house, the house where I grew up.

The house itself seemed a smaller place than I had remembered. All my family had left long ago. The house had been bought by a family that still lived there and had generously invited me back to look round it while I was attempting to write my autobiography.

They greeted me, this family of strangers, and going indoors I was taken aback by how diminutive everything seemed, how dark. What had they done? The answer was they had done very little. Here were the rooms I knew so well – yet did not know any more. It was as if, like Alice in Wonderland, I had suddenly grown larger and could hardly fit into these tiny yet still-recognizable rooms. Here was the miniature morning room with a telephone the never rang until my grandfather became ill (I thought of it as the 'mourning room' after he died there). But now it seemed a cheerful place, something we had not known. The kitchen, where my aunt used to read aloud to me, was equipped with a bright oven and impressive cooking materials that would have astonished us. The hall, where our huge television had presided, was now a comfortable sitting room with a fire where you could settle down while time drifted by. The Holroyds had used that fire only at Christmas – it was a present we gave ourselves, the present of warmth, as we pretended that the winter was almost at an end while knowing that it wasn't.

We went upstairs, but I did not want to examine what had been our bedrooms, now occupied by family ghosts. Instead I was asked whether I had ever as a child let down the ladder along the ceiling of our first-floor landing and as an adventure climbed into the attic. I never had. Nor did I remember the ladder tucked away on the ceiling. It must have been out of bounds and full of things that we had no wish to see again: things belonging to an unreachable past or a threatening future – sad things one should not destroy but cannot use. This attic was our oubliette.

But now that the house belonged to another time and a new family, it seemed appropriate, after their long hiding, for these forgotten objects to reappear and reveal their secrets. We climbed up there and I was handed a box of dusty photographs and two strange-looking volumes concealed behind old sheets and blankets.

The more substantial of these albums was a brown calf-bound volume some 18 inches in length and 12½ inches wide. Written in gold lettering on the spine was the single word 'Ferns'. On the front cover, which had become detached from the rest of this volume, was a rectangular gold line framing both the cover and three letters in gold: 'A.E.H.'

THE FAMILY

My great-grandfather Charles Holroyd was born in the autumn of 1822, the third of seven children. He passed much of his adult life in the Military Service of the East India Company in Upper Assam, retiring rather suddenly and unexpectedly in his mid-fifties with the rank of Major-General. During the Indian Mutiny in 1857 he had gained local fame for having unravelled a plot by Indian mutineers to massacre all the Europeans in the province. The tea planters in his area presented him with a large silver salver inscribed with their gratitude for saving their lives and gave him shares in their plantation – shares which were later passed down to his second son, my grandfather.

Charles Holroyd's domestic life was ill-omened. At the age of forty he had married a widow who died of apoplexy within nine months of their marriage and towards the end of her pregnancy (their child did not survive). He brought up her two sons and then married again nine years later. His second wife was the third daughter of Delia and Thomas Smith, a sugar manufacturer or an indigo planter or simply a gentleman, depending on which of his three daughters described him in the registers of their marriages. The youngest of the three daughters, Anne Eliza Smith, was born at Chinsurah in West Bengal, some twenty miles north of Calcutta, on 2 August 1849. She married Major-General Charles Holroyd on 26 August 1872 at St Paul's Cathedral in Calcutta. He was in his fiftieth year, she was twenty-three. It was then that he gave her as a wedding present the book I am holding, with her initials on the front. I open it carefully, turn the pages, and begin looking at a most extraordinary gathering of Indian ferns.

The wives of British officers in India occupied their time aesthetically, drawing and painting the landscape, studying botany and arranging flowers, knitting and making clothes. They kept an eye on their ayahs (the Indian nurses) who were keeping their eyes on the children until they were old enough to be sent to Britain for their education. This was often the pattern. For Rudyard Kipling these years of schooling in England away from his parents were deeply unhappy. But Charles Holroyd, who had been born in Hyderabad and then 'sent home' to an English school, did not suffer such unhappiness, partly because his large family was divided between the two countries.

He attended the East India Company's college at Addiscombe in Surrey in the 1830s. This seminary was described as 'a militarized public school'. The cadets all wore uniforms (there were at any one time 150 of them, all in their teens) and they could be seen every Sunday marching to the parish church in Croydon. They were taught artillery, fortification and engineering as well as mathematics, chemistry, natural philosophy and languages (Hindustani and French). The East India Company had gained control over much of India – a massive territory ten times the size of Britain. This led to their employing a private army to protect their business concerns: trading cotton and saltpetre, silk and tea – and also opium, which was sold and exported to China. Unlike most public schools, Addiscombe administered no corporal punishment. For disobedience cadets were shut into what was called 'the Black Hole', where they were fed on bread and water (their prison being named after the notorious Black Hole of Calcutta, where in 1756 a number of Europeans had been imprisoned, many of whom died before the East

India Company surrendered). The cadets at Addiscombe were not particularly well disciplined and they enjoyed perpetual warfare with the citizens of Croydon nearby. Charles Holroyd passed his final examination at the age of seventeen. He was then free to return to Assam as a young officer.

The marriage of Charles Holroyd and Anne Eliza Smith was to be divided between the two countries. Anne seldom came into contact with the India of famine and disease – she lived behind the walls where the British recreated almost to the point of parody the culture of their homeland. The North-East Province was one of the least densely populated parts of India, but there was a diversity of creatures in the forests – tigers and elephants, bears and rhinoceroses. The rainy season lasted several months and the soil was extremely fertile. Less than half the province was cultivated but the chief commercial products came from the tea plantations, from some rubber-producing trees and from the blue dye that was obtained from the leaves of the perennial indigo which Anne believed her father planted.

But the large calf-bound volume her husband had given to her was occupied by ferns. These flowerless plants have a complicated net-like vascular system. When mature they scatter hundreds of microscopic spores into the air and in damp soil they germinate into small scale-like bodies known as prothalli. In India they filled the shady places and were said to have an advantage over coloured flowers because the beauty of the fern was lasting while that of multicoloured flowers was ephemeral.

I have seen several pictures of ferns which the army wives 're-planted', fixing them on to rectangular pieces of paper which were framed and hung on the walls of the officers' barracks and of their family homes. They make pleasant enough pictures, bringing the outdoors indoors. But none I have seen possess such ingenious designs, so intricate and imaginative, as those that Anne Eliza created. It is as if these ferns had been taken from their pastoral elegy, with its premature death and unfulfilled ambition, and transferred to a legendary paradise beyond the triviality of time. Anne Eliza had the eyes of an artist. On to the first twenty-seven pages of the book which I am holding, she has, with great patience and precision, stitched into a variety of patterns all manner of ferns. Well over a century old now, they appear miraculously well preserved, as if this has become their natural habitat.

Ferns were among the most ancient of plant forms that had started growing upwards from the primaeval sludge. Their lacy fronds had been adapted so as to let light pass from one layer to another, maximizing the low light shaded beneath the taller ferns.

Nearly all the ferns in this book are Himalayan species, almost certainly collected around the old hill station of Darjeeling, where many British families spent summer holidays away from the heat of the plains. Among the numerous varieties Anne Eliza collected were the maidenhair fern (*Adiantum*) and several genera (including *Dryopteris* and *Asplenium*) which later became familiar in British gardens. Her sewing of these fronds into her book is almost invisible; giving an impression that the ferns themselves are growing naturally across the pages. But what is extraordinary is the way in which she has designed them and the beautiful patterns she has been able to make. She starts ambitiously on the first page with seven colours of ferns – green, olive, beige, and shades of brown and yellow – arranged like a star with seven beams of light and the centre made more solid with an eighth fern planted above the others. At the back of the page you can see the cotton stitching – the same colour as the page itself – with which she had attached them.

On the other pages she tries out varying designs and patterns. Sometimes she uses a single fern, stretching its shape across the page. At other times she presents elaborate combinations of ferns with complementary shapes and colours, gold and silver, one across the upper half of the page, the other below, one light, one dark, as if indicating day and night, summer and winter. These pages are full of surprises. A number of the compositions are simple and bold; others more elaborate. There are ferns lying obliquely on the page with a fragile echo or shadow of small fronds positioned in the corners of the page. There are ferns encircled with an oval framework of small leaves. Together they seem to summon up an entire landscape.

Collecting and pressing ferns became a huge craze among the Victorians following the Crystal Palace Exhibition in 1851 (the royal fern, *Osmunda regalis*, almost disappearing from wild places). It was after this public spectacle that so many wives and widows of the soldiers in India took up this pastime. Anne worked at her *Book of Ferns*, with several mysterious intervals of blank pages, until she and her husband sailed to England towards the end of 1876.

She had passed what must have been these intervals in Calcutta where, in the summer of 1874, she gave birth to her first son, Charles Patrick; and where, in the autumn of 1875, my grandfather, Edward Fraser Rochfort, was born. She was again pregnant in the summer of the following year – and that winter she and her husband started a new chapter in their lives at a house called The Links in the Meads district of Eastbourne, near the ominous Beachy Head.

My great-grandfather, Charles Holroyd, and his children in the 'fernestry' at
Eastbourne in about 1885. The elder boy, Patrick, stands at the right of the picture.
Fraser, who was to become my grandfather, sits on the ground, a tennis racket in
his hand, while Norah perches on the back of her father's chair. The ferns in the
background are *Dryopteris filix-mas*, the common male fern of Europe, perhaps
with some small narrow *Blechnum spicant*.

Her daughter, christened Norah Palmer, was born in Eastbourne on 30 January 1877. In the box of photographs I was given at Maidenhead was one that had been taken at The Links. My great-grandfather sits on the left of the picture, bald and white-bearded, looking at the camera with a subdued expression. To the right of the picture stands his elder son, Patrick, and on the ground sits my grandfather, Fraser, with an idle tennis racket in his hand. Both boys are dressed in sombre suits and waistcoats, Eton collars and dark ties. Neither of them is smiling. They are on duty. But above them all, at the centre of the picture and perched on the back of a chair on which her father sits, is Norah Palmer, his daughter, my great-aunt. She looks more natural, more alive, than the others and is more individually clothed, with a grey pleated skirt, soft white trimmings at her cuffs and a lace ruffle with wide sashes. In the background, to the right and to the left, are what appear to be ferns growing up the sides of a conservatory. It is what the Victorians called a 'fernestry'. This photograph is like a shrine to Anne Eliza Holroyd, Queen of the Ferns. But she is not there.

I go in search but cannot find her. It is as if she never existed. Her name does not appear in any letter or will and I do not remember my father or grandfather mentioning her name while I was growing up. In the hope of finding her I turn to her two elder sisters, in case their lives can point me in her direction – and eventually they do.

At the age of nineteen, Janet, the eldest of the three Smith sisters, gave birth to her first child, a daughter, who died within a month of her birth and was buried in Calcutta. Janet's father had been born in Glasgow and so had her husband, John Stewart Paul. The two of them, husband and wife, decided to leave India after the tragic death of their daughter and go to live in Glasgow. It was there that their daughter Helena was born and then two sons, the younger one being named Charles Holroyd Paul. This name illustrates how close the Smith sisters' families were.

The second of the Smith daughters, Mary Anne Rochfort, had married an engineer in London who was twenty-three years older than herself and preferred being described as a gentleman. His first wife had died at the age of thirty-one, their single daughter having predeceased her. Mary Anne and her husband, Robert Humphrey Sears, lived at Taunton in Somerset, where she gave birth to four sons in six years. Then, like her younger sister, she seems to disappear.

I turned next to the deaths, divorces and remarriages in England and Scotland and was sent two extraordinary replies. On 11 February 1880, at the age of thirty-two, Mary Anne Rochfort Sears committed suicide by drinking carbolic acid, used for household cleaning, at her home in Taunton. A month earlier, on 7 January 1880, her younger sister, Anne Eliza Holroyd, then aged thirty, had also committed suicide by swallowing carbolic acid. Anne Eliza died at 29 Arlington Street in Glasgow, where her uncle William Smith and his wife lived and where her elder sister Janet also stayed with her husband.

For several weeks I felt that I had been travelling towards Anne Eliza. I never saw a picture of her, but her *Book of Ferns* had come so familiar to me that I felt I was beginning to know her. This awful suicide of the two sisters by drinking a caustic disinfectant and burning themselves to death was like the loss of someone close.

Anne Eliza's family did not blame her husband. All the evidence shows that they remained on good terms with him. Two days after Anne Eliza's death Charles Holroyd became 'the informant' on her death certificate, describing himself as a widower whose residence was 'out of the house in which the death occurred'. On 10 January she was buried in Lair 59 of the Glasgow Necropolis: 'The Beloved Wife of Major Gen Charles Holroyd'. Several members of her family were to be buried with her in Lair 59, including her mother, Delia, her elder sister, Janet, and John Stewart Paul, Janet's husband.

Whether Charles Holroyd was in Glasgow when his wife died or whether, as seems more likely, he travelled up there as soon as he heard the news I do not know for certain. Nor do I know if her two sons, then aged five and four, and her daughter, who was two weeks short of her third birthday, travelled to Glasgow. It seems likely that after Christmas Anne Eliza had gone up there alone to see her Scottish family in the New Year and that the young children, looked after by their governess and nurse, the cook, a parlour maid and housemaid, remained in Eastbourne when their father travelled up to Glasgow.

A darkness, rather than guilt or blame, seems to have hung over these two tragic deaths. Janet's first daughter had died within a month of her birth in Calcutta. Robert Humphrey Sears's first wife had died in England at the age of thirty-one (following the death of her only child) and this was followed in 1880 by the suicide of his second wife, Mary Anne, at the age of thirty-two. Charles Holroyd's first wife had died in the first year of their marriage, when she was pregnant. All this tells us how dangerous giving birth could be for many women in the nineteenth century and also how difficult it was for them to avoid giving birth to more children than they wanted.

In the preceding years the middle Smith sister, Mary Anne, had given birth to four children and the youngest sister, Anne Eliza, to three children. I do not know whether either of them was again pregnant at the beginning of the 1880s, nor do I know if the middle sister too travelled up to Glasgow at the beginning of that January so that all three sisters were together for the New Year. But I believe that the two younger sisters probably suffered severely from postnatal depression and that it was the prospect or danger of having another child that led to their suicides.

Charles Holroyd must have witnessed his wife's illness after she gave birth to Patrick, her first son, and may have attributed it to the painful experience of a first birth. But her depression after giving birth to her second son, my grandfather Edward Fraser Rochfort, persuaded him to bring her back to England (as her eldest sister, Janet, had returned to England after the death in India of her first child). At Calcutta Anne Eliza had lived under an alien sky, which her husband may have interpreted as occasioning or increasing her low spirits.

Did her three children know that their mother had killed herself – killed herself because of her children? Certainly everyone in the family would have wanted to protect them from such knowledge. I do know that my father, who spoke to me about his family, had never heard of his grandmother's suicide. Even without such knowledge Anne Eliza's children suffered from the absence of a mother – and none of them suffered more severely than the youngest of her children, her daughter, Norah Palmer. She may instinctively have apprehended something of the truth, having inherited some of her mother's dangerous sensitivity. Charles Holroyd's two sons went to boarding schools, then into the army or up to a university. But their sister stayed at home. Her father did not marry again, but employed a governess who became 'a companion' for his daughter and was in charge of her education.

Looking again through this *Book of Ferns* I see it as a coded autobiography. Anne Eliza entered the first long series of ferns on the pages during an early period of her marriage. The blank pages that follow indicate the months after the birth of her first son. She began again on regaining her confidence and happiness; then stopped once more after the birth of her second son. This pattern was repeated when she and her husband came to live in England, the blank pages following the birth of her daughter and then fewer and fewer pages of ferns added with less skill. Then nothing. She committed suicide because she felt herself to be failing both as a wife and as a mother.

The Ferns

A varied cross-section of genera and species. In the centre a curving green frond of *Selaginella involvens*, which grows atop a stiff stalk on mossy rocks or moss- and orchid-laden tree branches. Anticlockwise around the outside, from top, slightly left: the yellow fertile frond of *Onychium lucidum*; a narrow-segmented *Onychium lucidum*; a branch of *Selaginella monospora*; at bottom, the rare *Lycopodium complanatum*, with its flattened branches; to the lower right, a pinna of a high-Himalayan speciality, *Athyrium decorum*, named by Professor Ching from Yunnan, China, but also found recently to be common in Darjeeling and Sikkim, usually above or about the forest tree-line. Then just above mid-right, another branch of *Selaginella monospora*; and finally, top right, a baby frond of *Polystichum longipaleatum*.

At the centre is *Onychium cryptogrammoides*, a high-Himalayan fern; the fronds surrounding it are all from *Selaginella pallida*, except for the one at bottom right, which is *Selaginella subdiaphana*. The two are quite different when you observe closely and I have the impression Anne Eliza might have known that and deliberately included a bit of variety in these fairy mosses (fern allies, not mosses).

In the middle of the centrepiece, the top fern is *Asplenium laciniatum* subsp. *tenuicaule*; below this is a very baby plant of *Athyrium distans*, an attractively dissect lady fern, abundant around Darjeeling; overlapping the athyrium's stem is a tiny horizontal frond of *Cystopteris fragilis*, which in India only grows up in the high Himalaya; and at the very bottom is a little frond of the higher-Himalayan *Athyrium flabellulatum* – a rather distant relative of the British lady fern, *Athyrium filix-femina*. Around the left side of the centrepiece, above is a frond of a baby plant of *Polystichum longipaleatum*, and below a small *Arachniodes coniifolia*. Around the right side, above is *Polystichum longipaleatum* and below is *Asplenium tenuifolium*.

The outside ferns, left side, from top to bottom: *Onychium siliculosum* (with attractive yellow sori); *Onychium vermae*; *Onychium siliculosum* (fertile form); *Onychium siliculosum* (sterile leaf). Right side, from top: *Onychium vermae*; *Onychium lucidum*; *Onychium siliculosum* (half sterile and more finely dissect at the base; half fertile at the apex). *Onychium lucidum* was discovered in Nepal in 1802 by the first British visitor to the then 'hidden realm', Dr Francis Buchanan, later Francis Hamilton, of Leny Castle, Perthshire, a remarkable botanist and zoologist who travelled all over India and Bangladesh, and whose gravestone has recently been restored and placed in the herbarium at Edinburgh Botanic Garden.

A whole page of different spleenworts. Centre: *Asplenium lacinioides*.
Left side, from top to bottom: *Asplenium lacinioides*; *Asplenium yoshinagae*
subsp. *indicum*; *Asplenium yoshinagae* subsp. *indicum* again; *Asplenium*
obliquissimum (a Himalayan waterfall fern). Right side, from top: *Asplenium*
lacinioides; *Asplenium obliquissimum* (two fronds); *Asplenium lacinioides*; *Asplenium*
obliquissimum (which was known to Colonel R.H. Beddome, Chief Conservator
of Forests, Madras Presidency, author of the *Handbook of the Ferns of British*
India, Ceylon and the Malay Peninsula, 1888, as *Asplenium unilaterale* var. *udum*,
a synonym, but in botanical nomenclature a superfluous name).

The centrepiece: on the left is a frond of *Selliguea griffithiana*, which grows as an epiphyte on trees around Darjeeling; in the upper mid part, a small frond of *Plagiogyria pycnophylla*, which grows near to Tiger Hill and Ghoom station of the Darjeeling Railway and could be picked shortly after alighting from the train at 2000 metres, in the cool mist after coming up from the baking hot plains; on the right is a pinnule of *Angiopteris helferiana*, a gigantic fern with wrist-thick stems and arching leaves 3 metres tall and 4.5 metres long, from deep sheltered gorges in the lower foothills.

Around the edge is a circle of a very rare club moss (an ancient fern ally), *Lycopodium complanatum* – not just the common *Lycopodium japonicum*, which can be seen woven into arches adorning village gates at weddings and other celebrations. In fact in five decades of fern excursions in the Himalaya, I have only ever seen it once, in Sikkim, at high altitude – about 2700 metres. Anne Eliza must have known it was special, I reckon, as she used this alone in the surrounding of the design.

The centrepiece: at the top, a leaf of *Cotus* (Nepali and Darjeeling), the Indian chestnut tree, with nuts like our sweet chestnut, roasted in autumn; bottom left and bottom right, trifoliate leaves of *Oisaloo* (Nepali and Darjeeling), one of the Indian *Rubus* species with yellow fruit that are nice to collect in the wild after the monsoon, and good to eat. The ferns between them are 'filmy ferns', with delicate translucent leaves one cell thick: top left, top right and bottom right are all *Hymenophyllum exsertum*, with quite long hairs on the midrib; bottom left is the delicate *Hymenophyllum badium*. They both coat the moss-laden tree trunks around Darjeeling at around 2000 metres upwards.

Around the edge is a ring of the little *Lindsaea odorata*, which smells of hay (coumarin) when newly pressed, like the Atlantic British hay-scented fern, *Dryopteris aemula*. *Lindsaea odorata* grows in masses on moist banks at 1800 metres upwards.

In the centre is an *Oisaloo* leaf. Around the surrounding circle, anticlockwise, from top centre: *Polypodiodes fieldingiana* (syn. *P. microrhizoma* of C.B. Clarke's *Ferns of Northern India*, 1880, written from his travels as school inspector for Bengal Presidency, including Sikkim and Bangladesh); *Goniophlebium argutum*; *Polypodiodes amoena*; at the bottom, the twinned tip of *Dicranopteris lanigera*; then a small *Polystichum manmeiense*; and finally a small frond of *Pteris normalis*, which has red stems when living.

Left column, from top down: a small frond of baby *Athyrium setiferum*; then the same again; then baby *Peranema paleolata* (a most beautiful, lacy fern when full grown); at the bottom, *Dryopteris dilatata*, from Britain.

Centre column, from top down: a baby *Athyrium distans* (abundant around Darjeeling); in the centre, a fertile leaf of *Bolbitis deltigera* (the pinnae are covered in a dense mass of black sporangia); bottom, another small *Athyrium distans*.

Right column: top and next down baby *Athyrium distans* again; then *Peranema paleolata*; then, bottom, another *Athyrium distans*.

In the centrepiece: at the centre top and right top are two small leaves of a baby *Peranema paleolata*, which forms huge, lacy fronds at high-altitude forest margins; the large yellow central frond is *Onychium siliculosum*, with its fabulous yellow-powdered sori; at the bottom, pointing up to the right, is one of the silver ferns, *Aleuritopteris albomarginata*, which has small winter (dry season) fronds with white powder or farina beneath; then the two little fronds pointing down at the bottom are, on the left, the Indian gold fern, *Aleuritopteris chrysophylla* (from the Greek for 'yellow leaf'), and to the right a small baby frond of the white *Aleuritopteris bicolor* (the most common of the Indian silver ferns).

In the surroundings, at the top middle is a baby sporeling frond of *Dryopteris cochleata*, and on its left and right, two sloping dark leaves of *Hymenophyllum exsertum*, a filmy fern that grows commonly on mossy tree trunks and curls up when it doesn't rain for a few days. Around the rest of the outside is a ring of *Aleuritopteris bicolor*, which grows through a huge altitude range, from 200 metres above sea level in the plains to 2600 metres or more in the main Himalayan ranges. This species leaves an imprint of a white powder copy of the leaf when slapped on to the hand or arm, and small children often pick it to play with when walking along the mountain paths on the way to school. Its smooth, shiny black stems, called *Rani-sinka* (meaning 'Queen's little stick') in Nepal, are also used to insert into an empty ring-hole in the ears or noses of village girls, where it apparently combats any infection in a new piercing.

In the centrepiece are three fronds: at left perhaps a small *Polystichum discretum*; in the centre a small *Athyrium distans*; and on the right a frond-apex of *Athyrium eburneum* (which is green when alive, but always dries blackish as you see here, hence the name, given in 1850 by Kew's blind pteridologist John Smith).

Around the outside is a glorious wreath-ring of feathery Indian fairy mosses, *Selaginella* species, *S. subdiaphana* and *S. pallida*, mixed, common in shaded undergrowth in the lower Himalayan ranges.

In its simplicity and framing of space, perhaps the most elegant of all Anne Eliza's fern pictures.

Centrepiece: at the top, *Athyrium distans*; lower left, *Thelypteris dentata*; lower right a small leaf of the very fine *Polystichum longipaleatum*, where the teeth at the leaf margins are drawn out into long, narrow hairs, and young uncurling leaves at the start of the monsoon look like bunches of hanging furry caterpillars, with tiny rain drops caught on the russet hairs.

In the four corner pieces of the frame: top left is a pinna of *Athyrium distans* and a small yellow frond of *Aleuritopteris chrysophylla*; top right is the yellow fertile pinna of *Onychium siliculosum*; bottom left, reversed into a mirror image, is *Onychium siliculosum*; and at the bottom right is almost the reverse of the top left, with the yellow frond of *Aleuritopteris chrysophylla*, but instead of *Athyrium distans*, a baby frond of *Peranema paleolata*.

A two-part design. Top is a fan of maidenhair ferns, actually consisting of two different species. The top three fronds are the common maidenhair, *Adiantum capillus-veneris*, named by Carl Linnaeus himself in 1753, the same species as the very rare British plant, confined to the south-west Atlantic coasts in Britain's colder climes. It has almost no teeth at the tips of the segments. The lower six leaves are the Himalayan maidenhair, *Adiantum venustum*, named from Nepal by Professor David Don in one of the first books describing a good number of the 1150 different species of Indian ferns, his *Prodromus Floræ Nepalensis* of 1824. This higher Himalayan species has a fan of many fine, acute teeth at the segment apices and a greyer frond with slightly striated segments.

The bottom group is a spray of the most delicate and finely dissect of the fairy mosses, *Selaginella chrysocaulos*, which grows in masses on all banks and small slopes of the upper-mid to higher Himalaya, from about 1800 metres altitude upwards to nearly 3000 metres. As soon as the autumnal frosts start after the monsoon the plants die down, leaving dried brown fronds and in the earth a small, pale subterranean bulbil, about 5 mm across, from which new plants sprout again to form a fresh green sward in spring. I reckon it would be good to grow as groundcover on banks in a British garden. I tried years ago in Wales, and the plants survived well enough through winters, but were not used to the dry summers – when they would normally be able to rely on the monsoon – so frequent watering was needed.

A whole plate of one feathery species, *Selaginella chrysocaulos*.

Here the centrepiece is non-ferny, but as it is composed of attractive variegated leaves that set off the ferns nicely, that can be forgiven! There is a tiny rounded leaf, probably of one of the many common Himalayan begonias, surrounded by white-striped leaves of perhaps a coloured tradescantia.

In the outer ring, from top centre anticlockwise, are: a young *Polystichum*, probably *P. discretum*; then a small *Dryopteris cochleata*, whose uncurling leaves are sometimes eaten as a spinach in the countryside in Nepal and Sikkim; then a dark frond of *Hymenophyllum exsertum*; then *Selaginella monospora*; then *Adiantum philippense* subsp. *philippense*, with its half moon shaped pinnae, which grows on old walls and dies down and disappears in the dry season after the monsoon; then *Selaginella monospora* again; and at the bottom, *Athyrium drepanopterum*, named after its sickle-shaped (*drepanos*, in Greek *pteron*, meaning a wing, or fern) upper pinnae. Then, coming back up the right-hand side: *Athyrium distans*; a tip of *Dryopteris sparsa* (the East Himalayan subsp. *rectipinnula* from its coarsely dissect, wide pinnae and lobes); a slightly mangled *Selaginella monospora*; a baby *Adiantum philippense*, now in two halves; and *Selaginella monospora*.

A single large frond-apex of *Polystichum discretum*, a species found in the lower-mid Himalaya.

A picture cleverly and almost seamlessly made up from ten different parts of the same species, common Himalayan club moss, *Lycopodium japonicum*, similar to and mistaken by nineteenth-century pteridologist authors for the European *Lycopodium clavatum*, but larger and with more of the spore-bearing 'clubs' or stalked strobili (not present here).

The centrepiece: at the top a frond of the thin, pale-green leaved *Acystopteris tenuisecta*; then, below left, *Athyrium distans*; right is a frond of a very baby plant which could be a *Dryopteris cochleata* or possibly *Diplazium laxifrons* (both common around Darjeeling); on the mid-right side is a pretty and finely cut epiphytic fern, *Katoella* (or, if preferred, *Davallodes*) *pulchra* (meaning 'beautiful'), which cloaks tree trunks in huge numbers; the lowest frond, pointing left, is *Asplenium tenuifolium*.

The ring of ferns around the outside consists entirely of *Onychium lucidum*, with its long, narrow fertile segments. The crossed fronds at top and bottom remind me of the universal Gorkha (or Gurkha) army symbol, the crossed kukri knives, which you see everywhere in Darjeeling (as in Nepal). The British Gurkha regiment was started by the Hon. Edward Gardner, first British Resident, or Ambassador, to the Royal Court of Nepal from the end of the Gorkha War in 1816. Gardner coincidentally was also one of the first botanists in Nepal who specialized in collecting ferns, which he sent down to be named by Dr Wallich of Calcutta (now Kolkata) Botanic Garden, and Professor Sir William Hooker of Kew Gardens. Many of the species in this book were first sent out by Edward Gardner to be made known to science.

The centrepiece is a beautiful placement of the pale-fronded *Selaginella chrysocaulos* set off in contrast against the surrounding ring of dark-fronded maidenhair ferns, *Adiantum capillus-veneris*, and *Adiantum venustum*. It seems like a pteridological depiction of a looking glass, framed by the maidenhair.

The centrepiece is a frond of the rather uncommon *Dryopteris pulvinulifera*, occurring in Darjeeling, mainly going along what is now Tenzing Norgay Road (named after Sherpa Tenzing of Mount Everest, or Sagarmatha, fame) to Aloobari (literally 'potato village') from the Chowrasta Square at the top of the town – it can be seen from the pony-back excursions along that road that still continue a century and a half later (as long as the pony doesn't manage to pluck it first!).

The outer surrounds are six groups of *Adiantum capillus-veneris*, the true maidenhair fern.

A picture in gold and silver ferns. The centrepiece has a largeish frond of *Polystichum longipaleatum* on top; a piece of *Selaginella involvens* in the centre; a baby *Polystichum longipaleatum* to the left; and a lowest pinna of *Onychium lucidum* to the right.

The outside ring is a superbly coloured arrangement of alternating gold and silver ferns (the yellow *Aleuritopteris chrysophylla* and two white ones, *Aleuritopteris bicolor* and *Aleuritopteris subdimorpha*), which keep their colour well for hundreds of years, as can be seen from old specimens in herbaria, as also here. Punctuation is provided by mosses (possibly *Thuidium* species) at the top and bottom and at the centre of each side.

A simple triplet of *Woodwardia unigemmata* in the centre; *Athyrium distans* to the left; and *Lycopodium japonicum* to the right.

A *Selaginella* centrepiece, with *Selaginella monospora* at the top, down the right side and at the bottom. According to degree of shade and moisture, this varies in form, in the crowdedness of its leaves and in colour, ranging through pale to dark green, strongly blue-green (in dense forest) and even a metallic copper colour (the colour variation can't normally be seen in dried specimens). There are also two smaller plants, left and bottom left, of the more delicate *Selaginella chrysocaulos*.

The ring around the outside consists of pinnae from *Athyrium decorum*, which may have come from the higher reaches of Mount Tonglo to the west of Darjeeling, on the Nepal border.

ACKNOWLEDGEMENTS

I am grateful to Aliette Boshier, Charlotte Edwards, Grace McCloud, Augusta Pownall, Rupert Thomas, Andrew Twort and the late Sarah Howell, Fine Art and Features Editor of *The World of Interiors*, for their initial encouraging interest in my great-grandmother's ferns; also to Pat Wolseley for her guidance on ferns. I am especially grateful to Jo Christian and Gail Lynch of Pimpernel Press, who came to see my volume of ferns and silent actors and decided to publish a selection of them. I owe much to the help of Richard Hollis, who introduced me to a magical memory stick, and especially to Angelo Hornak, whose brilliant photographs of my ancestors' work turned a far-off dream into these twin books which Anne Wilson has guided into this handsome boxed set.

Martin Rickard and Christopher Fraser-Jenkins have brought to my book of ferns a dexterity and scholarship which has greatly pleased me and, I am sure, would have delighted my great-grandmother. Her early death was a tragedy, but these pages of ferns show her happy days; and the twin volume, a book of actors, is mainly comedy. Together they exhibit the ups and downs of family life.